Christi N. Warner is a Namibian-born and theatre practitioner. She was awa~~_ _ _ _ _ _ _ _ _~~ Theatre for Development from King Alfred's College, Winchester, UK. In Namibia she worked for the non-governmental organization Bricks Community Project where she used poetry and theatre as tools for community empowerment.

She co-founded Township Productions Theatre Company, organised and facilitated creative writing workshops for young writers, served as the editor of *Poetree* magazine, co-edited the Namibian poetry anthology *In Search of Questions*, published by Basler Afrika Bibliographien, did freelance work for the *New Era* Namibian newspaper, Committed Artist of Namibia and the Namibia Ministry of Education, Arts and Culture.

She became a popular Namibian face and voice taking on many different presenting, directing and acting roles, one such role (Lady Makossa) for the Namibian Broadcasting Corporation. She was invited to perform her poems at the University of Namibia, various festivals, conferences and official events in Namibia and abroad, including for the First Lady at the Namibian State House.

She can now be seen performing in Oxford, UK. If she's not showing people how to walk with her poetry and dissect it, she's usually learning to appreciate complex LEGO designs, teenage fingers practising virtuoso Chopin on piano, making voices for cats and frogs during bedtime stories and mastering cooking like a proper Italian wife.

ICE
CREAM
and POLITICS

CHRISTI N. WARNER

Lucia, Giovanni and Alice
this gift is a piece of my heart

Contents

Foreword

Ice Cream and Politics is a worthy addition to the growing corpus of Namibian poetry. Christi Warner's anthology explores several significant themes including, gender roles in Namibian society, the scourge of gender-based violence, the complex nature of love, the vulnerability of children, the quest for identity and intergenerational tension.

As a feminist, Warner challenges Namibian society (and the world at large) to address the problems posed by outdated modes of thinking and behaviour that blight the lives of women and men, cause anguish in people's lives and relationships.

Warner's mastery of imagery and symbols provides fresh insights into the lives of the poor, marginalised and voiceless in an African setting, that nonetheless resonate globally. The collection of poems challenges the reader to re-evaluate his or her assumptions regarding the norms that govern life. A distinguished singer, a striking feature of her poems is the manner in which the words flow melodiously and her fascination with language itself. The cadence of several of the poems is rhapsodic. Her diction foregrounds the importance of visual imagery and her verse abounds with crisply delineated individuals whose struggles at times mirror the reader's experiences, or provide a lens through which he or she can broaden his or her sensibility.

Ice Cream and Politics is her début collection, which showcases Christi Warner's mastery of rhythm, reveals her deep-rooted concern with social justice and the broad range of her sympathy as she explores what it means to be human. A number of her poems were published in anthologies of Namibian poetry, such as *In Search of Questions* a collection of new Namibian poems, which she co-edited with Volker Winterfeldt and Keamogetsi

Molapong; and *Poetically Speaking* an Anthology of African Poetry. This anthology bears eloquent testimony to Christi Warner's talent.

Prof. Mbongeni Z. Malaba
University of KwaZulu-Natal
Durban, South Africa

Acknowledgements

A warm thank you goes out to my husband, Michele Cappellari, who believed deep in his heart that these poems needed to be free. Who worked tirelessly to teach me LATEX and helped with the layout, editing and design of the book. Thank you for motivating and inspiring me.

I am grateful to Mbongeni Malaba and Volker Winterfeldt, whose heart and soul went into the growth of these poems. You have been excellent friends and mentors. Thank you so much for your support and patience. Mbongeni, a special thank you for the foreword, it is a wonderful mirror to look into.

Matilde Cappellari, when I saw your first art work I was moved and that admiration never left me. Your image brings my cover to life. I'm looking forward to our next project. Grazie di cuore. Panos Lampridis, the cover is outstanding! Thank you.

Gwen Lister, I had a dream: I found a bottle of ink labelled "Gwen Lister's altruistic mentality." That aroma inspired my mind and the ink without a doubt filled my pen. But a secret ingredient I call magic whispered, "I can teach you how to shape this world but it's your heart that will lead you to action." Because of you I believe I can make a difference with my writing. Thank you!

Athol Williams how wonderful it was to meet you here in Oxford and to witness you performing your award winning poetry on stage. Thank you so much for adding my poetry on top of your many study duties. Please keep inspiring me with all those awards.

Dan Holloway, thank you for the inspiring words. When I first moved to Oxford, you and Kevin Jenkins helped me find my place and purpose as a poet and musician in Oxford. I thank you for your encouragement and support.

Tinashe Mushakavanhu I can't believe we still have not met. Your talent for detail has come in quite handy, thank you for your editing advice on my poems.

Tom Minnie, your eyes and ears on some of my poems, especially "Breaking Down the Fourth Wall", and "Play the Guilt Card" have been indispensable. Thank you.

Janet Remington, thank you for helping me sort out the reviews. I'm lucky that I can count on you here in Oxford.

Margaret Warner, when I was little and found it difficult to express myself, you told me in your motherly voice, "if you don't know how to say it, write it down." I believe that inspired my passion for writing poetry. I thank you for always encouraging me and for literally making sure I had the space and privacy to write my thoughts down.

To all my friends and family (close, in Namibia, Italy and on social media), you showered me with enthusiasm, time and encouragement. I am very lucky to have people in my life I can count on. Thank you for your advice, especially with regards to the title and book cover.

Some of these poems were published in the *New Era* Newspaper, *The Namibian*, *The Namibian Sun*, *The Republikein* and on the blog of the Year Zero Writers (WordPress). The poem, "Painting for sale" appears in the stage play *Black coffee, white porridge*, by Keamogetsi J. Molapong.

I am forever indebted to the founders of Bricks Community Project, Kitso Poets, Ama Poets and Molapong. These organisations and people have given me access to the real people who in turn helped me plant and water these poems.

Dear reader: thank you!

Part I

Personal

MY VOICE

One night she said
She said what little she could
"Mummy I wonder how the snake leaves its mark on a page
Today I saw a book and it owned my name.
Did the snake leave her mark in my name too?
My teacher is a magician, she took a wand,
tickled the paper and like magic it owned my name.
I just told her I'm SHEILA.
And for the first time I saw how I appear on paper.
Mummy will you teach me how to make my name, please?"

Darkness and daylight danced many times
She kept asking and I kept whispering,
"tomorrow, tomorrow sweetheart."
When tomorrow came, cooking kept me hostage
Cleaning kept me yearning for more time with her
but work became my child
And my child, a child of her peers, her teachers
Oh, how I wished to sit at her bedside and have my voice
paint the pictures in the storybook she kept on her bedside table
Oh she kept asking and I kept whispering
"It's too late sweetheart, you need to sleep,
tomorrow, tomorrow maybe"

Last night she said
"Mum, I'm a woman now
Will you be my witness tomorrow, it's my special day"
And I said "tomorrow sweetheart, it's a promise"
When tomorrow came she was my angel in white
On a piece of lawful paper she signed her new name
right next to the name I gave her
The same name I could never teach her to write
Sadness filled my eyes but just for a second though
because this day danced with pride
as she witnessed how I commanded the paper
to own my voice for the first time.

KISSED BY THE LIGHT

A canvas of struggle feeds my eyes
Vacant gorges of wrinkles tell of happiness now moved on
A closer look and I can almost sense
Pain on a mission to erase this man's existence
For a minute there
I see him drowning in a rip current
Waxed like a balloon in anticipation of a cheerless ending
Seconds after, my hunger for understanding
incarcerated like a suicidal fish on a hook
"Step back, step back"
Glazed eyes directing me
into the magnetic grey light
Like a river of calm
My worries fade into the realisation
Here's a soldier
Finding calm in a storm

MIRROR

You are the clinging mud on my perfect shoes
The coffee stain on my silky white dress
The screaming pimple no foundation can conceal
But you stand tall like my guide to history, I confess

You are the dark, sly dungeon that ignores my innocence
The calm, silent, alluring pond that shelters piranhas
The tormenting crossroads
that got me shaking my head
Yet the answer to vanished times, I confess

You are the thunder that barks when I'm scared
The lost key that mates with eternity
The sharp prickly thorn that makes a nest in my soul
But you are the lost piece of this puzzle that I am

You are the accidental blow of a hammer at work
The monthly bill that keeps me on the run
The mad whispering fire
that threatens my house to ashes
But you are the seed that made me real, I confess

You are the menacing winter ice that burns my fingers
The cantankerous germ that feeds on my diluted veins
The boastful cockroach that deserves a smack into darkness
Yet identity plays mirror with you and me

FINDING CALM IN A STORM

SS Andrea Doria, is that what I'm rushing to be?
No, my precarious future will not plummet into 1956
My captain's hat is still on
I know I can steer my ship

Oxford skilled I've always been – or so I thought
Made captain top of my class
Had all my lessons safe and packed
Found a toxic adventure,
became a seeker for more
Trainspotting followed
Got me stuck in this stark reality
Trepidation and faith danced my adrenaline high
I felt like Tony Montana – unseen scars in my veins –
Dancing with fame, too busy to see the danger zones
By chance making you feel good about your distinction

SS Andrea Doria, is that what I'm rushing to be?
No, my precarious future will not plummet into 1956
My captain's hat is still on
I know I can steer my ship

Now, I'm right in the eye of the storm
Please let your lighthouse shine on me
This calm cannot be trusted
I still have some lessons saved and unpacked
But let's be honest, I won't be unharmed
Wishful thinking if you thought otherwise
If I'm wretched
Close enough to touch the face of death
I have faith I'll rise like a Phoenix
And like the dust of St. Mark's bell tower
I hope that one day my screw-ups
Will fade under the light of my success

SS Andrea Doria, is that what I'm rushing to be?
No, my precarious future will not plummet into 1956
My captain's hat is still on
But I'm counting on AA and twelve steps to steer my ship

THE COLOUR OF NOTHINGNESS

I have not contemplated an agenda
No suicidal mission
Neither is this a declaration of guilt
No need to hurry your worry
My thoughts are a rainstorm
there's a chance of a flood
I have to get it out
so my brain cells won't drown
Feed it to my loyal pen
Ask it to paint this hopeful white paper
with the blazing words rushing from my brain,
eager to feed my mouth and hopefully your eyes
I have a waterfall of thoughts
Maybe keep an open mind
Or bring an extra cup
I'm quite phobic about making a mess

I'd like to talk about the darkest matter
I know this is not the time or place
But it never is
It comes unannounced anyway
I'd like to think of it as a kidnapper of essence
A disastrous scene no one can run from

Have you ever heard them say,
"He kicked the bucket peacefully"?
What could be so peaceful
about the suffocating drama of blackness?
It's a colour so controversial
Ask apartheid about this colour
Ask me 'cause my skin
was born the colour of these words
My eyes will tell you I'm a harmless fool
And you can't judge these words
by their colour, this colour

Anyway, I consider this dark matter
a notorious untouchable gangster
Whom you sign a contract with the minute you're born
and with time you see its power
Mocking you by stealing the ones you love
Smirking at you, a dancing finger pointing at you
Scaring you almost out of your socks
Leaving you with just enough breath
to ask God for help
Don't ask me why, my colour is my nature

If you ask who's a coward
Three little fingers will tell you who
I'm bone and flesh, with a heartbeat
To kick the rhythm on my chest
so you'll know I'm human
I'm just like you,
three little fingers will tell you how
One minute you caution those who condemn you
after that you do the attacking
then you ask God's forgiveness
Don't ask me why, my colour is my nature
Three little fingers will tell you that
You'll sing the same song, next!

COLD FIRE

I allowed my ear to play stethoscope on your chest
Just to be mocked by false notes
Now I know that's the sound of your heart
It's amazing because from a distance
your glittering teeth promised me
a heart filled with angel voices
But now I know the truth
You brought me hope from China Town

Cold Fire, that's what I'm faced with
Cold Fire, I could never imagine
A cold fire, life's got issues
but at least I know you're just a vicious cold fire

I was all alone,
Performing trapped fish in a fish tank
In the distance I saw your inviting grin
I was hopeful, even the water felt my trust
Like water and soul we danced the ripple dance
Little did I know grabbing onto your paw
is a promise of my end
Now I know even a smile can bamboozle me

Cold Fire, that's what I'm faced with
Cold Fire, I could never imagine
A cold fire, life's got issues
but at least I know you're just a vicious cold fire

I abandoned my blanket
Took your advice to keep your fire company
From a distance the crackling of the wood
and the golden melodic sparks
eased my shivers into a calmer dance
Just for a second though, because a close-up
helped me face reality
that my blanket would have been a better friend

Cold Fire, that's what I'm faced with
Cold Fire, I could never imagine
A cold fire, life's got issues
And now I know you're the dealer and I'm the addict

REFLECTION

When blue waters shine like a mirror
My eyes paint a vision the colour of water
The colour of dust, lonely dust
When I look deeper into it
I see a broken heart, a jaded soul
I see traces of a familiar façade
It must be my fairy!

So, don't ever say:
I'm the face of loneliness
Don't even think:
I have no friends

When the blue waters shine like a mirror
My eyes paint a vision the colour of water
The colour of dust, lonely dust
And when I look real close
I see the face of love,
the wink of hope,
the smile of tomorrow
I see no fairy, but I see the one to trust

Me, myself and I

SWAHILI[1]

In Swahili there's a saying
The Word is broken English
In Swahili there's a saying
A master key can dance with many locks,
Serviceable to the thief
A hindrance to the home-owner

In Swahili there's a saying
the world is small it's just a ship
Take your first flight out little bird
You will fall, I promise, you will
And when you do, your wings will learn

My speech is a bullet, but listen

Come on out little bird
Don't hold back face your fears
I understand your predicament
but your nest is not the whole world
Spread your wings 'cause they're meant to fly
Shine; ask the star what's her secret
Dine, but with caution, for this world has many flavours
Fear is your friend, but don't let it detain you
You'll be fine you're so much stronger than a porcupine
Believe; says the word of God

---

[1]A version of this poem appears in the musical album *I Found My Rhythm*
by Christi Warner.

In Swahili there's a saying
that the Word is broken English
In Swahili there's a saying
smooth seas don't make you skilful
In Swahili there's a saying
the shy tortoise died in a boat
Take your second flight out my baby bird
You'll fall harder, I promise you will
But now you know, your wings can spread

Sometimes love is a bullet, but listen

Fly away little bird
Don't come home until you're strong
Find me a leaf on top of Kilimanjaro
No more sorrow for what's over
Long gone are the days when you thought
You won't see the clear blue sky
All it took was to turn the key
And there you are
Standing braver than Jumbo the elephant
Like a child of the universe
Like an Angel on a swing
Bringing promises of sunshine, like a weatherman

THE SONG OF BOB

Here's a story of a boy named Bob
Bobby-Bob had a vision he had a dream
He had a guitar and named it dream maker
He told his ma, he told his pa
And they started his song with na-dee-dah
Go get yourself a jobby-job, Bobby-Bob

He took his bud down Independence Avenue
Where he sat and played
His tunes were harsh, his sounds were hungry
But beautiful too and just so real,
it would slow you down if you were in a rush
Smiley faces and dancing heads
Some just clapped, made their feet rock
to the rhythm of the African vibes
that cascaded from each string
All day long the crowd stopped to give him an ear
But were their hands too busy to dip inside their pockets?

He told his ma, he told his pa
They brought back the chorus: na-dee-dah
Go get yourself a real-real job, Bobby-Bob

He met this man, a producer
Honey dripping from his lips
"Hey Bobby-Bob let's make some cash"
With words so sweet how could he resist?
(Little insect feet caught in a web)

First music studios, then radios, then TV studios
Bobby-Bob was the man with the dream
A busy bee and an instant market hit
Even newspapers gave him a temporary home
The ca-ching ca-ching kept on flowing in
And just like magic turned into an 8-room mansion
And a golfer's car for the honey dripping man
Bobby-Bob scratched his head
Coins never made it to his tattered jeans pockets

"You don't have the skill to make money rain,"
Said the man's big fat tummy
that not so long ago sang the song of the hunger march
"If you put all your bricks in building questions
Your songs will never stir wisdom like Great-Zimbabwe
The streets gave me a bagger, with bubblegum talent
I gave you a face and a voice that should climb mountains
My kindness equals time equals value
and for that you must pay
No one else really want you – without your fame
You think you want to leave
There's the door, hear these dancing keys
I'll gladly open it when you can shine in the light"

He told his ma, he told his pa
and they ended his song with a sad-sad tune:
Go ask fame for food and a roof
It might just believe in a magic guitar
that invites coins to disappear

AUDITIONING

Who am I?
I guess 'I' am that shell reflected in the mirror

Mirror go deeper, show me my emotions
Emotions, be my sprinter, help me feel who I am

Am I so lost that I can't feel that smile?
Smile, shine and bring my face to life

Life of mine believe that smile, please just try,
Try to connect that smile with my eyes

Eyes wide shut,
Shut the images that scar my soul

Soul resounding with the rhythms of lies ironical echoes of
        dreams I've lost
Lost in the maze that promises the path to my heart

Heart of mine, awake and take the lead
Lead me; prepare me for this big role

Role the red carpet under my weary feet
Feet that'll dance a routine until I resurface

Resurface like leaves on the trees in spring
Spring, an artistic and wow phenomenon

Phenomenon for the doubting heart and human mind
Mind that still chooses to see, not to believe

Believe 'cause life breathes even in a tree wintry dead
Dead and dull I cannot remain when my dreams scream to
              be alive

Alive is the word that will fire up my monologue today
Today is the day I vow to be the best at playing me

BECOMING HUMAN

Twelve noon I'll dissect courage with the Obamas
Write a script with her pen
Borrow his divine voice
to move hearts and mountains
Learn the mechanism required to hold on
to a first-class dream in the quivering world
Of Dr Martin Luther King junior

I'll ask fear to break its principle,
when it feels my heated distress
Whisk me through time right next to Rosa Parks
Allow me to witness the essence of a winner
even when trepidation remains dominant

A sprinkle of Oprah Winfrey's self-less scent
A moment to rest in her empowering shadow
Will help prepare me for the test
on the path to become supreme human

Ask me a synonym for merit
My mind will scan you an African lion
caged in Robben Island
I wonder will I ever ignore my innocence
just to stand for a cause?

But then again
I once ripped through the brain of a Kenyan man
And fed myself his optimistic and cultured philosophies
Of how I love to stand up strong and believe in the power
to move the centre and be the lifeguard of my vernacular
And then I screamed at the top of my lungs:
"I will marry when I want."

Ngugi wa Mirii's teachings are as perennial as the grass
He showed me how to let my voice
continue auspiciously when tomorrow comes
to erase my human body. Even when at times
it feels like I'm "howling against the wind"

When I feel trapped
I remember "why the caged bird sings"
A lonely yet sanguine tune I keep hearing
My own land taught me the same striking song
Maya Angelou, I know my own liberty's in reach

Tsitsi Dangarembga
You are the female worrier in me
The force that can allow me to stand tall
When my feminine world seems to lose its identity
And threatens to become energy with asymmetrical power

Ostrich hold my head high like Winnie Mandela
When humiliation threatens to swallow me
Help me stand from the dust and fight back
Maybe I should visit our own son of the soil
And ask him to teach me the skill to hold a striking smile
Even when our country's caught in the midst of a frying pan

I felt peace when the little white dove flew over me
I know famine will rob many of the true essence
and beauty of the peaceful white bird
Madam Wangari Maathai, every time
I see the poor smile I can't help but think
You've showered them with hope

My Saturn, so becoming you are
Who else can show me
how to identify the divine affection
that God encrypted in you and me
Your ring strengthens my identity
and this mad craze for our family
You've become my daily guide which helps me tap inside
and indulge my soul into the most powerful human emotion

Tonight, when my trusted old pillow comforts me
I'll stand with Dante and Shakespeare on a stage
And find hope for this skill I adore
When the rich stroke of the morning light wakes me
I'll be packed with all diligence
ready to see the madness, touch beauty
Listen beyond the pain and taste laughter

Part II

Emotional

FEELINGS

I feel my intuition signalling harsh emotions
I sense a dark mood threatening to destroy any sign of bliss
There's something real urging my feelings to find a voice
But if I follow the brave road to verbalisation
I could get lost and burn my tongue red and dry
I might make you run like a headless chicken, scared
Might make you brawl like the king of the jungle, mad
Maybe direct your feelings close to a scene at a coffin, sad

Or worse of all
make you walk tall
Right out of my life
I can't take that dive
I might feel like an old seal
ruined with a knife

I feel there's something I have to shout
I don't know how, but I must let it out
So please, just give me the space
To whisper these feelings that feel like a maze
These beliefs filtered yet bewildered
Will my prose coldly mark you as its senseless host?
Maybe sting you with naked cruelty?
Words of passion yet fake novelty
Words of anger, with undue slander
But my intention will never be to fry you in grief
So please listen; let my kindness be your thief

I feel there's something
I have to paint with red swollen tears
I don't know how, I don't know what's coming
But I must face my sullen fears
And will my words to emulate the mood
Of a stern and candid, yet warm and kind violin key
Just will my words to become what your soul needs for food
Really will my speech to become the magic dust that'll set us
        free

Free to fly us high into loving each other completely
Free to rescue us from the magnetic pool of uncertainty
Fear is good sometimes, but evil when it attracts destruction
And now I cannot let it win my affection
Today my heart will bleed my truth
Honey might be sticky and messy
But I hope you will remember it's a real treat too

WAYS OF THE DESERT

I had a dream about you and me
At first we'd meet as friends
Though secretly I was hoping
We'd be more than just friends
And that you were hoping that too

At first we'd be like tourists
Exploring the desert of an unknown country
With just enough to survive
For the days we had counted

Later, these days
Would not be in our vocabulary any more
We'd explore the desert as two on a Sunday drive
And with nothing to worry about

Also we would not notice
Our victuals steadily vanishing
Relieving us from the weight
And when there's just enough for one
Selfishness will be at hand
And we will scramble to save ourselves and not each other

Last but not least we'd meet as acquaintances
Knowing deep-down that we are enemies
Promising never to make the same mistakes again
And yet jealous of new partners

And at the very last we'd be like children
Who learnt the way of the desert
of an unknown country
Though secretly perhaps we would be hoping
To break the ice between us
And meet again as friends

HOPSCOTCH

Hear the story of a young man who was never happy alone
Yet all his life he was a loner
His mummy lovingly swaddled him
then dumped him in the arms of a dark church door

Daily, his peers at the orphanage
painted portraits of happy families
while his nightmares teased his hand
to paint an image of an old man and his dog

Twenty-three years of uninvited solitude followed him to a
        restaurant
where he tried to acknowledge his birthday
And just before he could make a wish
The candlelight did a vanishing act

When he looked up
His heart played hopscotch staring at the vision at the door
Her eyes found the empty chair next to him
And her rambling stomach eagerly invited her into his life

They made a collection of passport stamps
Lived in and out of suitcases, in hotel rooms with pompous rats
Sometimes burdened a friend's comfy couch
A lifestyle engineered to attract only cheap labour

She told him "your fancy degree will build you riches,
but I won't let it fix me into a motionless empire"
Oh, she had him by the tie
But she also scared solitude away

In a little town that looked like a reverie of home
they settled longer than ever
A dream job lured him like a fish to a hook
His birthday memory harked back, good things do bring change

She came home that night champagne in one hand
his heart in the other. Naturally it was her moment
She finally found her calling in another town
His wine glass made a cowardly toast

Solitude poked like the devil on his shoulder
She loves him? Maybe enough to stay?
Possibly she'll understand
Conceivably she'll know his dreams matter too

Her suitcase screamed "you lost her"
He took her to the train station
Too empty to host a tear-drop
he turned with just one wave goodbye

In their favourite spot at the park he welcomed back solitude
He looked up and the shooting star was gone
With wilting shoulders he got up,
forced acceptance clearly through his lungs
When he turned, his heart played hopscotch,
Inviting her weeping eyes back for a promising start

THE PINK ENVELOPE

The postman's not winning the slug race today
It says seven past on the friendly old kitchen clock,
The school's rusty gates will soon fly wide open
Seven is my age and he should have been here
I'll hide my letter one more day
Hold it tight between my heart and pink vest
Make sure my smell stays trapped on its pages,
Mummy once said I smell just like strawberries
I'll let my fingerprints remain more visible
than that of the postman
so mummy can have all the clues to find me

Marcha says two is smaller than ten
She's convinced years come and go like lightning
The frown on my face is hope and fear
I can cheerfully count the seconds
between thunder and lightning
But it's annoyingly scary watching two winters stretch
Reluctantly I wore the laborious heat of two summers
And autumn already stripped the Jacaranda trees twice
Oh no, I can't take another spring away
from the Lavender fever-berry smell in Mummy's hair

Another summer will come
and Marcha will say, "three is far from ten"
You know that too don't you?
My age says I'm seven
but I already know
she's just playing the big sister game
She always has a clever answer
I wonder what she'll say when we reach ten

The golden sun has already woken up
I'm still seven and I can count till twelve,
the friendly brown kitchen clock taught me how
I know it's almost time for the school routine
Auntie likes to wake us up
with the smell of sour porridge
One hand feeds me and the other
holds the daddy man's black cane ready
Just in case my stomach decides
to feed the black and white chess floor titles
Marcha's brown eyes, always ready to leak when it happens
I guess she thinks she can help me clean the kitchen floor
Maybe I should tell her to stop
there's no need for both of us to get a beating

I can tell auntie enjoys our pain
Oh, she hates it when I call her auntie,
but my loyal head tells me
if I can't have Mummy now
her name is what I'll hold on to
That's why aunty can't have it,
not even the daddy man's cane
can rob me of Mummy's name

The doorbell announces the coming of the awaited
I know it's him; no one dares to visit this early
The kitchen clock must be reading my mind
Seven loud strikes announce my excitement
He won the race today
I know this time my letter will find Mummy,
the postman promised that he won't rest
until he finds my mummy in the desert
"that's why I'm a postman," he always says
and then deposits me a wink for assurance

I rush to the worn-out black security door
just in time to witness how it swallows
the tall grey body of a faceless somebody
dressed in the postman's uniform
"What happened to my postman with the big smile,"
I ask him and it could be that he didn't hear me
His tongue carries a seriously different lingo
and the frown on my face tells him
my ears have not yet been introduced to his sounds

I know the school routine will start real soon so
I'll take a chance and trust this postman's uniform
I deposit a little pink envelope
in his big unfriendly claw
And in broken Afrikaans
he complains about a missing stamp
and no post box numbers to guide the destination
The old postman never asked me
for a stamp or numbers to guide him
This one must be new on the job
Before I can answer him auntie rushes in
and speaks some magic words,
which makes his claw hand her the pink envelope

Marcha's off to school
I'm locked in my temporary blue room
Auntie said I need to learn what prison feels like
Hate has only four letters,
not far from two, so I'll study hard
So I can find ten letters to show how much I hate her
My body's painted with purple blue stains
Dressed in my birth suit
I can see every mark, every design
I couldn't even save the pink envelope,
auntie read it aloud in front of the faceless
postman and I couldn't jump high
enough to stop her from uttering the witch's laughter

She knows my secret now
soon the daddy man will know it too
The faceless postman left without my letter
My letter disappeared like my trusted postman
like the kitchen with the friendly old clock
like the school that taught us the abc
It disappeared like auntie
She also stole the daddy man's car
the stuffing of the daddy man's shop
she kindly left him the bright yellow walls
and the dancing keys in the door

The sun has already woken up
I am eight now and I can count beyond twenty-four
We're in a new house
without the friendly brown kitchen clock
We have a new auntie
When the daddy man goes off to work
she'll be three sheets to the wind
too busy to pick up the cane
or interfere with my plans
We have a new postman
He likes to show me his gap teeth
I've started to write Mummy another letter
Soon I'll know the postman's routine
I attend a new school
My teacher talked about the desert today
I know now where my letter should go
Marcha stole a stamp from her teacher's desk
She says we shouldn't worry because:
"three is far from ten and Mummy will find us"

HIDE AND SEEK

"Daddy's playing hide and seek again"
said little Penda and immediately
charged his tiny feet to find the door
Leaving little sis and mum
to keep the modest backyard company

"Daddy, daddy where are you,"
questioned his six year old voice,
moving from room to room
He looked in the kitchen, the lounge, the privy,
oh just about everywhere,
even in little sis' room, in his own room
But there's one room he did not attempt
and that's Mum and Dad's room.

"He would never hide in there" thought Penda,
Mum's stern finger seems to agree,
occasionally she plays back in his mind,
especially when he stumbles over the "Do not" list.
At 6 he is already trained to think before he acts,
thanks to Mum. Not the pain-enduring head of little sis,
still friends with the back of Mum's hand

He looked everywhere,
this time his body set on rewind
Always best to look again,
you never know you might have missed something
But soon he realised Dad was nowhere

"That's strange because
he did not deposit his footprints
on the front stoop today,
not even in the little backyard,"
his modest brain cells commented,
trying a hand at problem solving
"No!" he warned his disobedient thoughts,
"Mum's room is off limits,"
But his thoughts became louder and louder

"No, no, no, shut up!" he yelled but
just as well he had to give in
because his thoughts took control of his little feet
Dragging him to his mum's room
Steering his petite right hand towards the door
"I'm innocent, I'm innocent,"
he yelled using freedom of speech
while his voice still had control

"There you are Dad," said Penda
Relief escaped from his lungs
"The one place you knew I wouldn't look
Mum's voice will reach Kilimanjaro
if she finds out you made me disobey her finger"

But then Penda realised
Dad wasn't in the mood to play the game today
Not in this forbidden room
In the middle of the room
Dad stood on a tired oak chair
with a menacing muscular auburn lash
decorated around his neck,
fed to him by the greyish white ceiling

"Dad, how long can you ignore our laughter
in the little backyard?
Come play with us,
we need you more than the ceiling,"
he pleaded letting mature thoughts
mark his face with a frown
"If the ceiling falls, let it
We can always buy a new one tomorrow
And if your bank is broken
we can always break my piggy bank"
And like a magnet, his little voice
made the desert rain in his daddy's eyes

Daddy's playing hide and seek again
and so is mummy, little sis and Penda
This time the game unfolds in the little backyard
and "the ceiling will fall but dad will be here
and together we'll pick up the mess,"
his voice proudly concluded

THE RHYTHM OF LOVE[2]

I'm not trying to be vicious
I'm not asking for an ideal world
That would just be too factitious
And I'm not dropping just another cliché
Wits say someone's got to keep this discourse going
If you want to pass this course
Facts don't rest with Adam and Eve
Just leave the past or you'll be deceived

The mission today is to fight for equality
In actuality that entails genuine action
Like push-starting a car up the hill
You'll hear them whisper
"Well, why bother, that's not my car anyway"
That's just bitter

Curiosity's got you going like a louse on my noise
'Cause this time I spit what's stored in your heart
I must be hinting silence
Compared to violence
Silence is just as crude
Dude I could lie but I promised to set the mood

---

[2] A version of this poem appears in the musical album *I Found My Rhythm* by Christi Warner.

When waters seem quiet
It could be that deep down
where the sound is bona fide
Trouble's winning an award for destruction
False love in protraction,
making promises but no action
Empty words sounding smooth
like African Boy's[3] verses

Passion portrayed in purple blue stains
She's in chains, but she's deceived
Who's gonna change her tire,
If she says it's over
He got her thinking she's a butterfly
Needing shelter from a tornado
Newsflash, her life is a vortex
Solitude scares her more
And so she stays in shackles
Making you and me believe
that those are jewels of love
Dream on if you choose to accept that

Talk about shackles,
fetters they be hidden too
It's sisters playing mould the clay
See how we play our artistic flavour on brothers
She can't find Mr. Right
But she sure knows how to choose her knight

---

[3] A popular Namibian Neo-soul singer, known for his silky smooth, heart
stirring vocals and lyrics.

She's got the craft to make him spot on
Her favourite game?
Put the puppet show on
And if he doesn't want to bend
She won't say nothing, feet stomping
Make him think their story is ending
Then give him the squint-and-stare

He will say nothing but repent
With Dolce and Gabbana maybe Versace,
Gucci, Truworths[4] if you're local,
come on girls the truth must be vocal
If he ain't got the loot, some chocolate will do
And when she's stout and loud
He'll have reason to leave or deceive her

---

[4] A South African clothing retailer with a branch in Namibia.

Brands and Bills
make life a game of traps
His game is lame
but seeks his fame
ready for clubbing
He's got his gear on
Stay clear 'cause the plan
is to dunk some girls
He made some bills
now he's revolutionized vellies[5] for Timbo's[6]
Walking like a star in a Katutura[7] music video
Jacob the jeweller's asleep on his arm
Been off duty since he nicked it off some tourist
It sure is big enough to charm,
no one will notice the battery's on strike

He's not sad, check out his mouth,
It's going platinum
Enough to make the girls go frozen
Jeez, how some brothers trap you
You're hooked like a fly to flypaper

---

[5]Veldskoene: Southern African lightweight, but extremely tough walking shoes, believed to be based on the traditional Khoisan footwear.

[6]Timberland shoes.

[7]Katutura is a predominantly black township in North-western Windhoek, Namibia established in the late 1950s under the white South African apartheid regime.

She's going on a date
She thinks it's fate
And yet she's late
He's gone out the gate
He ain't coming back
his heart is black
The game is on
he's got another fool for loving
Maybe another bun in the oven
Will she sue? What's the use,
he ain't got no money honey
She had no clue
And now she's blue
Quick, bring a scoop for her cone

Show the other side of the coin
Come on girls, the truth must be vocal
She got burnt 'cause she thought
she could get this mountebank fat cat trapped
But he ain't got no money, honey
Rush the ice cream, a bucket will do
She's just so blue

I got food for thought
But I know when to stop
I might just find myself
on the wrong side of the sword
Lord, save me if this precision causes a riot
Amen

FAMILY PORTRAIT

Precious moments
Come like thunder and lightning
But too often
Sadness and fear steal the frame
Tear-drops, our link
As you watch me grow
hope remains your faith
You spend all your time
playing lifeguard in the rain
I don't care, it seems
And now that I'm grown
you feel you don't belong

In this family portrait you belong
If you're the missing piece,
my puzzle is useless
Just remember without you
There'll be no portrait
Your eyes, your smile,
your love make a difference
So much more that I remember
Without you life won't make sense
No family portrait
No family portrait

I don't say this often – I know
I can see the dust hanging on every word
You deserve to be part of my speech
In fact here where I stand
You are my actions, my stories,
my memories and possibilities
You are my blanket and because of you
I'm winning the heart of my own warm house

In this family portrait you belong
If you're the missing piece,
my puzzle is useless
Just remember without you
There'll be no portrait
Your eyes, your smile,
your love make a difference
So much more that I remember
Without you life won't make sense
No, family portrait
No family portrait

WHEN YOU HAVE TIME

When you have time
please lend me your mind
I promise you no word
or phrase will be erased
I won't even take a chance
to lose a single sign
Just like an analyst
I want to know how you manage
to tickle my ears with so much wisdom
Every time, you shower me with words
I feel like the queen of humanity
If anyone throws question marks at my cheerful face
I tell them it's because I know the finest architect
who shared with me the skill to build my character
dream up a castle and make it real
The skill to see myself amongst the stars
and not to forget to face the mirror
I know one thing for sure,
In you I've found the cure to sorrow

When you have time
Please lend me your heart
I promise to return it
with every single beat
With my stethoscope
I would like to uncover your unique vein
The one that knows the true meaning
of the word unconditional
Every time I share with you
something gloomy and soiled
You always manage to help me see
that the dark night
just like the day has a purpose
Whenever I share my fears with you
You always help me see the winner in me
What blows my mind every time
is how your heart makes me believe
that I am Cinderella
rescued from a crazy resistance

When you have time
Will you lend me your eyes
I cross my heart
you'll have them back
I know how important a function they have
Would I keep them
with what eyes will you view
and enjoy the fruits of your success
How will I ever enjoy that amorous look again
Everyday I dream of our first encounter
My heart remembers
feeling like a Leonardo da Vinci painting
And everyday I keep seeing my true reflection
The hidden truth as you see me
The hidden truth that you've helped me feel
So you see why I need to lend your eyes
I'll tell you this much
You won't trust a mirror no more
Your eyes will teach me how to paint the truth

When you have time
Will you lend me your hands
No scratch or pain will haunt them, I promise
In my dream I thought I saw Idi Amin's hands
But when you came real close
Your hands felt like an angel's breath
Like little white feathers dancing on my skin
Leading my body into a pleasure dance
Now I know what to ask you
Share with me the secret of your sensual touch
The secret inscription I believe
is hidden in those creative lines
Left by God in the palm of your hands
I ask you to share with me the skill to read my own
Payment will come when I return the favour
I'll tell you this much
Whenever I want to feel like silk
I close my eyes and lure your touch to my hungry flesh

When you have time
Will you lend me your lips?
I promise you'll have them back
Sealed with all the tenderness
and love you've entrusted me with
For just a minute longer
I'd like to step outside this dream
And in this time of marvel
I hope to discover
the secret recipe that they possess
Every time I hear your sounds vibrate
through that magic world
My heart leaps like the finest gymnast,
Oh how beautiful your lips part
to make meaning of a simple word "ciao"
Please lend me those lips
that bring me thunderous bliss
I can almost swear
I feel heaven every time our lips meet
So, will you part from them - just this once
So I can find that secret recipe to create magic
I promise you this
When you have yours back
You'll know that I've learned from the best

THE AVALANCHE

A hammer knocks violently on my heart
My tears are an angry flood
My mouth produce an ocean of confusion
Emotions are raw
They've been too long unspoken
I'm broken, you're heartbroken
You're a statue with human ears
Crude words hit you like a speeding drunk driver
Your frown is a screaming red light
Then there's the slam of the door
Makes me fear it'll stay shut for good
I know it's hard to see my cold side
But I don't have the strength to pick myself up
I feel myself slipping down
This mountain we've build
I scream, you're alarmed
You throw me a rope
I react like a sloth
I'm desperately in need of you
You jump down, I'm a feather
I feel you cushioning my quivering body
It silences the fear and awakens hope
I'm stunned by the pain in your eyes
I don't want to win this fight
If it means you have to lose your smile
I can't promise you less cloudy days
But I hope when it rains
We can stand strong under one umbrella

Part III

Social

LESS ORDINARY[8]

An ordinary sunny day, working day for me
I passed this house. Just an ordinary square
with an ordinary fence - made of ordinary wire
With a keen desire to help me see this
Old woman, sitting staring at the distance
Where she left her mind
Six months now: less ordinary if you think

I turned, and said hello! First time in six months
First time in six months she found my eyes
I rescued her from the distance just for a second though
The longest second I've ever been bestowed with
And in this little time I saw something more
I felt something more
I am convinced
'cause my jaw almost touched the dusty road
Less ordinary – if you think

An ordinary sunny day, working day for me
But I couldn't pass this house. I had a keen desire
to step behind the fence made of ordinary wire
to say more than hello to this
Old woman, sitting staring at the distance
Hoping that maybe she'd help me see
what was further down the street

---

[8]First published in Molapong, K. J., Warner, C., Winterfeldt, V., eds., 2005. *In Search of Questions*. Basel: Basler Afrika Bibliographien.

I found the gate, my behind found an empty drum
My hand shamelessly found her shoulder
– an ordinary gesture
Again she found my eyes and this time I had a smile
but not as old as hers not as warm as hers
"He's coming home," she said
"They say the heroes have all come home
Not all true, because he's still coming
The 21st of March has not yet reached him"
She seemed convinced 'cause her eyes danced with hope

She spoke of how the war was raw
and how he had to leave with the heroes
in search of peace
I knew the salt had left my eyes
when her hand tried to soak it up
Then and there I knew too that my 26 years of peace
in this land of the brave
had not yet begun for this old woman,
sitting staring at the distance
Her hero had not yet returned
But "he's coming home," she said

An ordinary sunny day, no working day for me
I passed this house. Just an ordinary square
with an ordinary fence – made of ordinary wire
which helped me see the reality of this
Old woman, sitting staring at the distance
26 years now: still waiting
for her war to end in this land with no war

ANSWERING BACK[9]

Callow is our trademark
conceptualised and caged
By your contracted view of our capricious moods

Hoodlum is the image that penetrates your logic
Every hour, every minute, every second
your eyes hover over our being

Retouching eagerly over our images
You recreate us to be a mere retrospective
recollection of your radiant times

Identical you want us
An ignominy so ineffable
Impossible to accept, inviting our insouciant response

Subjugate the sinister to the senile
Scrupulously you sabotage our chance
of self-control

Torpid under your totalitarian rule. Hatred becomes possessed
and seeks refuge away from the trauma which then
causes a turbulent trend and declares war against the taboo

Immaculate you believe yourself to be
And declare your innocence. Sanctimoniously,
you unfold your pride and dress us up as iconoclasts

---

[9] First published in Kgobetsi, S. E. I., ed., 2000. *Poetically Speaking*. Windhoek, Namibia: Gamsberg Macmillan.

UNTITLED YOU

Stand in line
Make sure you can prove your eminence
Oh and don't forget proof of past suffering
Where are your marks, your pain?
Do you have a story to tell?
Does it involve guns,
rubber bullets, and tear gas?
What about dik[10] Damara[11] stones?
Sleeping with the silent in trenches?
Or was exile your fate?
Nothing?
I'm sure you know the tune
of some political song?
No?
If not, sorry because
Your suffering has just begun

---

[10] Afrikaans meaning for thick.
[11] An ethnic group that make up about 10% of the Namibian population.

PAINTING FOR SALE[12]

Ladies and gentlemen, and the auction begins
Gently lend your eyes to a much darker side
A deeply hidden side
Fine-tune the chords in your ears
For a sound so hollow and sweet
That knows the touch of bitterness, pain and shame
A world of questionable silence
I ask once more
Allow the hands of pain and shame
to mislead you to reality

The artist shall remain a puzzle
Not the Who, but the Why
The image portrays provoking colours
Brings us back to the path of shame
Let's zoom in on the eyes – her eyes –
They speak of loving fear
Her peach lips speak of praise
Yet tremble at the thought of him
The silent crimson shadows beneath spell out pain
louder than the words that pass her provoking lips

---

[12] Previously published as "Battered Paintings for Sale" in Kgobetsi, S. E. I., ed., 2000. *Poetically Speaking*. Windhoek, Namibia: Gamsberg Macmillan.

What magnetises you most
Is the variety of colours
that bring the final touch
to this million-dollar piece
But most provoking
are the burning blue stains on her sensitive skin
The artist shall remain a puzzle
But it's his art that tells the story of an Ogre's work

       Going once
              Going twice
                     Sold to Anger and Shame
                            And now the talking starts

We move on
This image is a work of art
Her shame brings out the best view
And instantly focuses on her pain
Pain that touches her everywhere
The prick that forced out her last bit of pride
Pride which once consoled her
Pleasure which once made her smile
A smile which once spoke of her audacity

This artwork brings out the goriest detail
Our eyes can feel the acquaintance with blame
They hunt down the reason for this gory picture
The warm blood in which she swims
The torn-down clothing
that pretends to wrap her sensitive skin
That pretends to hide her stained beauty
from questioning eyes

What magnetises you most
Is the variety of pain and silent screams
That brings the final touch to this million-dollar piece
But most provoking is the thought
Penetration without her consent, without consultation
A treasure – painted forcefully
to quench the thirst
of his rigid narcissistic masculine muscle
The artist shall remain a puzzle
But it's his art that tells the story of an Ogre's work

    Going once
        Going twice
            Going…
                Going…
                    Gone!

Where it shall remain to tell a different story
For the buyer shall open it up to the world to see
Sold! To Anger and Shame
and now only hoping that it's much talked about

LOST IN THE FOG

She makes love look like thick fog
Breathtaking at first sight
Like a child I was mesmerised
I was anxious to let her in
But my heart was a forgotten tin
still hoping to be filled
"I'm your puffin," she promised.
"You'll never have to evict me"

So I let her rent a room in my heart
Now her words are that wrecking ball to my wall
I've learned to crawl for her warmth
With my wrists in chains, she screams:
"you're that toad no one but me wants to kiss"
Her silence, a heavy pillow on my face
I'm much safer in her violence
But her soft hands around my neck
Tastes power and control
With every practice run

He makes love look like thick fog
I feel a highway crash coming on
He's so in control, he's out of control
Oh God help me

Tuli's line[13]
Hides the flaws of Ray Rise on my face
A regular hexagon understands equality
But all I get is a systematic apology
He knows he's got my loyalty
I've got to put my face on
Or I'll never see the sun yawn
I feel the human in him calming my quivering body
This gentle security rushes away doubt
Then his tongue kicks me off balance
"Clip your wings or my desperate heart
will chase you into the dark night"
I've long packed my suitcase
Waiting with bated breath
for empty threats
to push me out of that propped open door

"Why don't you just leave"
Said the mad mouse to the home owner
"You have no backbone"
Boasts the carefree grasshopper
"You must have provoked him"
Said the wasp in his most waspish voice
"Just be obedient next time"
Said the donkey matter of factly

---

[13]Namibian manufacturer of natural make-up and other beauty products.

I live in a fabulously normal world
Band-aid solutions
Often come rushing through my door
I turn to the girl in the mirror
Her words cut like a machete
But at least she's not telling me
To put my naked hand in the beehive

POVERTY

A contagious germ that causes division
The hatchery of egoism
The instigator of jealousy
The pillager of pride
Ever-so-often
the base-line of the pessimist's song

The notorious thief
that robs many of higher learning
The demolisher of dreams that could have been
The homeless know its cruel intentions
And daily the news can afford to rank famine lower
Than the jokes of the missing million dollars

But there's hope in the stories of the humble few
who managed to escape this wrecking ship

TEACHER OR UNDERTAKER

I'll meet you, I'll meet you not
I'll meet you, I'll meet you not
Oh help! Confusion's got me hostage

Failure, will you tell me the secret
How do I meet your enemy
without falling prey to you?
How will I recognise your enemy,
if I'm afraid to face you?

I'll meet you, I'll meet you not
I'll meet you, I'll meet you not
Oh help! Confusion's got me hostage

Please spare me your frustrations
How did Nujoma get that smile,
if he never kicked your ass?
How did we regain this land
if we still face your colonial threats?
How did Heroes Acre become a hero's home?
Did they donate blood to drown your threats?
How did our flag get to dance so free in the wind?
Did it step on you to get that high?

I'll meet you, I'll meet you not
I'll meet you, I'll meet you not
Oh help! Confusion's got me hostage

Please spare me some regret
With her anger she stabbed him
His passion pushed her into a shallow grave
A mother drowning in solitude
Wrapped the umbilical cord around her frail body
Forced her little body in black for the garbage collector
A father pleaded with the unknown
Was he afraid to let his child meet you
When he shut his baby's eyes for good?

Newspapers are flooded with such atrocities
Is this your face? Are you here to take me down?
Why do we seem to be so confused with your existence?

It might sound safe to stay in my cosy egg
But just like a bird ready to embrace life
I know I must break free from your shell

HER WISH[14]

Once upon a time, you made a wish
A wish to be innocent
until you find the one
The owner of the rib you carry
You'd join the circle of love as one
And now we'll know if it ever came true

She too made this wish
She was happy, very happy
This one day she met him
In his eyes she saw her future
Felt quite safe when he asked her to dance
Oh, they danced the night away
Soon it was time to go
but he wouldn't let go
He wouldn't let go
No, he wouldn't…

Now here's a little twist
To him she would say
"Be me and I'll be you for a second
Feel my hands loosening you from gravity"
But definitely no soft landing
Cuts and bruises all over her skin

---

[14]First published in Molapong, K. J., Warner, C., Winterfeldt, V., eds., 2005. *In Search of Questions*. Basel: Basler Afrika Bibliographien.

Take 2: see these hands
tear what covers her skin
Pushing her legs apart
Forcing silence to escape her lips
See these eyes,
enjoying every moment of her pain

Now you know the truth
Pain and fear rent a room in her heart
Stalking her every day,
'cause she knows
My wish was vain

THE IMAGE ON A PICTURE

It was a morning in June
When my eyes weak and heavy
shook hands with heaven's light
Shivers danced my body with no rhythm, no control
As a cold blanket of air crept under my needy attire –
of long gone summers' threads

Happy thoughts can bring warmth,
I heard my notions whisper
As the reminiscence train went back a decade
Window dressing my earlier childhood
Filling it with manna from heaven
A wardrobe for every season
While grandma's laughter filled the plate
And mother's heart sang me to sleep

Mother's eyes swam in care
Hiding exhaustion and pain
Her paper dry hands and ballooned feet
unfolded the story of a cleaner
for three miessies[15] in town,
Rewarding? Yeah, apparently
Just enough for grandma and me
Just enough for our monthly roof
Just enough to warm a lean feast for our hungry insides

---

[15] Afrikaans word that derives from Madam. A common way maids called
their female white employer.

Hard work paid mother and grandma's one-way ticket
Hosted them in a yard under a thick blanket of gravel
And left me a child of the stars
A loner, living in dark alleys
I explored the taste of drought, eating rich
From one buffet to the next
Warmed up and garnished by the stench that creeps
inside the greedy piggy bins of every restaurant

A voice carrying rude bags of pride
Pulled me harshly into the present,
Painting the image of an angry pedestrian
Making my doubting self prepare for war
Prepare to confront
It was not what he said, so rudely
But his face…
An image that stepped out of a picture I've kept
A treasure mother gave me
Finally the streets of the city
brought us together

Suddenly, I heard fear conquering his voice
As a woman touched his hand, lovingly
Afraid she'll discover his eyes in mine
He forced her kindness back into her pocket
And pulled her away from me
I felt the hands of anger taking control of my heart
as my eyes tinted with the selfishness that framed his
The same selfishness that deprived me
from grandma's laughter and mother's heart

Like a slovenly paragraphed sentence
Omitted from a page
hosting concise explanatory sentences,
I accepted my ordeal as a loner

SON OF THE SOIL

Son of the soil
Your tale has been told
Captured in the hearts and minds of many
Your tale swims oceans of books
Remains still in statue mode for tomorrow's faces

Son of the soil
You played a tune so sad
It danced through the bars of your prison window
Touched the hearts of many
Yesterday you reached out hoping to salute a hand
But no free hand could find yours

Son of the soil
You were robbed
You stood trial
But you still took the Lion's throne

THE IDEAL LEADER

He is light as a feather
But on solid ground he stands – come any weather
He never sees the wind as a destructive evil
But rather as a means of travel
He is akin to the traveller floating without purpose
But if the truth be told that's to be close to you and me
He is light as a feather
but beware of his strength – he's an ogre
He is firm as the root of an aged oak tree
Yet will grant you shade and home – perhaps a permanent key
By the ingredients of power he is capable of filling your plate
But he will never spoon-feed you or threaten you with being
          devoured
He has the heart and vision of the chosen one
But cannot resist a chance of a duel – like Don Juan
He is the head that we all want to proudly carry around
But she is hard to find

THE CONE EFFECT

I took a selfie, seductively
demolishing my divinely
gooey pistachio ice cream
and the ice cream maker
made mad money
he's bringing his
bulldozer to
evict you
I wish I
asked
him to
pay
me
first

PLAY THE GUILT CARD

I like vanilla ice cream
It began with my mother
Daddy learned to respect it
My children will learn to worship it
No chocolate or wild new flavours
Will seduce my loyal heart
When you hear mother tell the story
Of the king who could not sleep
Your heart will desire only vanilla

He was mad, I tell you comrade
If your body dared to dance the doze
he would sing into action
"off with his head"
Those who loved separation
Thought he was sane

Grandpa had a plan:
"we can make ice cream without a fridge"
Those craving the sweet taste of freedom
Thought he was insane
But blindly put their faith in his coarse hands

Secretly grandpa gave all children cream,
lots of vanilla and sugar in plastic bags
With rock salt, ice and cold hands
They danced all night, all day
Rubbed, rubbed until the ice cream came
And the wicked king
Who had no ice cream
Became bony and frail
Faced the music
Followed that deep sleep certain to us all

This plot-line might seem a bit wonky
Don't worry, there's a core to this story
You don't eat under my roof, I know
But in nineteen ninety
you put the crown on my hero
So vanilla ice cream
Should be your obsession
Put your brain in detention
Bring your heart to the table

Dear reader:
limiting believes are a set-up
Your vote is your voice
it's your choice
so step up

ROSES OR GOLD

I live in the era of Job Amupanda
Where silence lives in fear of extinction
I can feel an eruption in preparation
My heart is in a whimper
Don't want my voice to become that hated twister
Don't want to force it down your ear neither
Please pull up a chair dear minister
Come down to my level if you must
Show your children you're here for them
help them see there's no monster under the bed
Look in the closet, you told them to trust you
How can they if you choose to stay in the hall and yell
"go to sleep!"

My parents are angry with you mister
The shadows on the streets are tenser
You've floored us with your decision Mr. Politician
I saw it raw in the good old newspapers
You just had to go and push that panic button
You plunged to make a decision for the fish
A monumental decision for the sea
You rushed a colossal decision for this land
Played judge and jury for my future

You had a scale in front of you
Had to choose between
a bar of gold and a field of roses
And it seems the scale screamed gold
I don't know if you know how much roses we really have
There are times we have to be open to the possibility
That roses too can outweigh gold

How magical is the dance of the waves
with the golden desert sand
How stunning is the strings on the guitar
of the tattoo wearing fishermen
I imagine they like singing
"we are the land of the lucky star pilchards"
I dream that one day I will swim
with our bottle-nose dolphins
I eulogise those mountains of salt at the coast
And can't wait to season my kapana[16]
Can you imagine your mahangu[17] without it?
Did you warn Air Namibia?
What will they do without the flamingo?
These are just some of our roses
When I grow up, I don't want to go to a museum
to show my children dead roses behind a glass

---

[16]Grilled meat sold at open markets in Namibia, cut into small pieces.

[17]Pearl millet, grown mainly in the north of Namibia because it grows better than maize due to the unpredictable climate.

I know you think I know the word Independence
from a song of Destiny's child
But fear not, I am well aware of our hero
The father of the nation
For me the synonym for independence
His story teaches me
Stand up for my beliefs
Because of our history
I put my hand on my heart when I sing
"Namibia land of the brave…"

Dear Minister
Please sit down
Meet my crippling fear
School me on this unsolicited change
Hear your children cry
help them see there's no monster under the bed
Call the ghost busters if you must
Look, as I'm pointing to my closet
Look, if you want our trust
Please just stop yelling: "go to sleep!"

You don't want to be the father of this land
Sitting on a chair, in a circle
twenty years from now
pouring her heart out
Talking about your neighbour, the monster
Who found a way through her window
and crawled into her bed

BREAKING DOWN THE FOURTH WALL

Casually he said, "come here baby
Let me lift your gloomy mood with butterfly wings
Come, my soulfully sassy lady"
Ooh, I like this high-risk name game - let's play
I sense I'm cute and cuddly
So I'll let you nurture me
Just don't push me too far into the flame
I'll roll-over, wiggle my tail and be your puppy

"You're more than that" he whispered
"The heart and soul of my universe
You're my queen bee
I was born to serve you, I cannot flee
I'll fill your stupendous heart with glee"
Queen bee! I see you trust me with your future spawn
I'm game, go on I'll let you feed me

"You're more than that" he bagged
"My snugly sexy bunny
Hop on over and let daddy spank you"
You tickle me with your word play
Here's your red velvet rope
Sit back, while I bring fame
to your Playboy mansion

"You're more than that" he winked
"You are my First Lady"
Ooh, such sensual words
might just warm up my bleeding heart
Come on Mr President
You've got the power to reinvent me
"Oh God," like a cub he growled
"You've got the power
You're my doyenne"

Now direct your mind out of their muddled bedroom for a
        minute. Will they ever learn to capture her essence?

What if Cinderella rescued herself?
What if her prince was the seat in parliament?
What if her evil stepmother was a worthy opponent?
Let's tweak this tale a little more
Dress up Poverty and Disease
As her evil stepsisters
Will she ever make them gasp with just her wits?
Will she let them grow like seeds in the rain?
Or do you believe they know they live on borrowed time?

If you've heard of a land
where the desert meets the sea
Where the sun shines proudly on a flag
Chances are you've heard her heartbeat whisper:
"Just sip on hope, like vitamins."

84

LET THE DRUM ROLL[18]

Sit back and hear my version of a phenomenal woman
Don't worry this is not a moment to duck and cover
An ambience of sadness is not on the list, I swear
But if maybe a tear-drop should fall
Keep reading and you'll soon find your voice

Silence has the scent of an angel's beauty
But stinks when it fades out the good
of a phenomenal woman's struggle and persistence
Her availability to assist grants her precedence
History had me blindfolded in an ignorant corner
But now there is a face to this honour

For instance, she is just like water
Flowing down the well of my thirst
Allowing me to drink from her feast of wisdom
She's got style. See I'm not talking about fashion
I know sometimes our eyes prefer to notice how
her designer labels steal attention in parliament
But in time our ears will catch on
and see how she walks the truth
Playing Shakespeare then Madam Wangari Maathai
To a forgotten poor, a hungry people

---

[18]This poem was written for and first performed at the event "women with
a mission," hosted by the First Lady, Penehupifo Pohamba, at the Namibia
State House in 2005.

She's just like a bright light
Allowing me to really see my dreams even in dark corners
Encouraging me to borrow some of her fire
It's amazing how she keeps going strong
Amidst these ghost voices that can't stop echoing the song
of the woman and the kitchen
You heard those voices too, haven't you?
But you keep going strong
See, now that is amazing
And doesn't it call for an ovation

Let the drum roll. Let the Drum[19] talk
Let You[20] walk her steps. Let Insight[21] see more
Sister[22], thumbs up! Let them know, you know
They see her sparkle on your cover

---

[19] A South African magazine aimed at black readers; containing market news, entertainment and feature articles.

[20] A South African magazine covering current events.

[21] A monthly journal published in Namibia which focusses on current political, economic and social affairs.

[22] Sister Namibia was first published in 1989. It is a magazine designed to inspire and equip women to make free choices and act as agents of change in their relationships, their communities, and amongst themselves.

I'm talking about ordinary women
A partner of the sun: she'll give you your wake-up call
Set the table in time. Jump to the next scene
Finding precision in the corporate world
I wonder how she finds the oomph
Then there's this wonder woman:
out of an empty cupboard
she feeds a family, even orphans
Her heart is the miracle
How can I not boast about this woman?

Heroes like this should flood historic pages
Pages in nativity. The birth of a deprived voice on paper
Captured to savour a phenomenal woman's existence
A phenomenal woman's struggle and persistence
It's amazing how she twists through the chains
Finding her beat in the noise
When I look at her shadow, I witness the art of pride
And I know that I have the potential to shine just like her
Maybe because I'm a woman too

I got food for thought. I'm a word kleptomaniac
Hitting you hard with Oxford words from my lexicon
Hoping you'll face the mirror and know
you are this miracle worker. Yes you!
Now help me echo this with precision

Let the drum roll. Let the Drum talk
Let You walk her steps. Let Insight see more
Sister, thumbs up! Let them know, you know
They see her sparkle on your cover

Also by Christi N. Warner
the music album
I Found My Rhythm

65820859R00058

Made in the USA
Charleston, SC
06 January 2017